Ben Franklin

Elena Martin

Contents

Rigby

A Harcourt Achieve Imprint

www.Rigby.com
1-800-531-5015

Who Was Ben Franklin?

Every country has leaders. When the United States was a very new country, Ben Franklin became a leader who helped plan rules that the people would follow. Ben was a great thinker, a funny writer, and a smart inventor. His ideas made life better for people in Philadelphia, Pennsylvania, and his life is still celebrated by Americans today.

honoring Benjamin Franklin's 300th birthday in Philadelphia

Ben Grows Up

Ben was born into a big family from Boston, Massachusetts in 1706. He had 16 brothers and sisters. Ben's parents couldn't pay to send Ben to school for very long, so at age 10, Ben had to go to work.

At first Ben helped his father make soap, but Ben didn't like the smell of the fat he cooked to make the soap. So Ben went to work for his brother James, who taught Ben how to print signs, books, and newspapers. Ben also learned that he had a talent for writing.

young Ben

Ben learned a lot from James, but the two brothers did not get along. When Ben was 17, Ben left for New York and then for Philadelphia. He even traveled as far as London, England and lived there for a while.

Ben liked living in London, but he returned to Philadelphia when he was 20 years old. Soon he had his own printing shop, a wife, and a baby. Ben loved to talk with friends about business, news, and ways to improve themselves and their city.

Ben's first visit to Philadelphia

Ben's print shop

Ben Makes a Difference

Ben loved Philadelphia. He thought this new city in an English colony should have the same good things he had seen in London. Ben started a club for people who wanted to make their community better. These people set up a city library, a free school, and a hospital.

Ben's club helped cover Philadelphia's muddy streets with stones. His club also helped the city set up well-trained firefighters and police officers to keep everyone safe.

city library

Ben, proud leader of firefighters in Philadelphia

Ben printed his own newspaper. It gave readers suggestions on how to make their lives better and keep their homes safe. Every year Ben also wrote and printed a book called *Poor Richard's Almanac* that gave information about the weather and changes in the moon. Farmers used this information to help grow crops. Ben also wrote fun sayings that made people think.

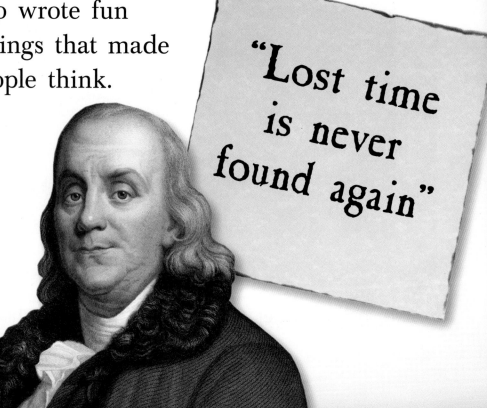

"Lost time is never found again"

Poor Richard, 1733.

AN

Almanack

For the Year of Christ

1733,

Being the First after LEAP YEAR

And makes since the Creation
By the Account of the Eastern Greeks
By the Latin Church, when ☉ ent. ♈
By the Computation of W.W.
By the Roman Chronology
By the Jewish Rabbies.

Wherein is contained

The Lunations, Eclipses, Judgment
the Weather, Spring Tides, Planets Motions
mutual Aspects, Sun and Moon's Rising and
ting, Length of Days, Time of Hi
Fairs, Courts, and observable Days.
Fitted to the Latitude of Forty
and a Meridian of Five Hours West
but may without sensible Error, ser
jacent Places, even from Newfoun
Carolina.

By RICHARD SAUNDER

PHILADELPHIA
Printed and sold by B. FRANK
Printing-Office near th

Poor Richard's

Almanack

Benjamin Franklin

pages from
Poor Richard's Almanac

11

Ben Changes America

Ben had many new ideas. For example, he thought that lightning had a special power that people could use. And whenever Ben thought of a new idea like this, he wanted to try it.

One story says that Ben flew a kite with a key on it during a storm. He felt a shock when the lightning hit the key. Ben thought that someday people could use lightning to make electricity.

Ben invented eyeglasses that helped people see better. Ben also invented an iron stove that was safer to use than a fireplace because it didn't cause as many fires.

When Ben put his mind to it, he could do almost anything!

Ben flying kite during storm

Many people in America wanted the English king who ruled their colonies to lower the cost of tea, paper, and glass that came from England. They sent Ben to London to speak to the king about unfair charges, but the king wouldn't change his mind.

Ben and other colonists decided they had to fight a war for their rights. With Ben's help, the 13 English colonies won the war and became the United States of America. They called July 4, 1776 their Independence Day, which is a holiday the United States still celebrates.

Ben died an American hero in 1790. He will always be remembered as a father of our country.

Ben at work with American colonists

Index